PIECES OF ME

SOULS INKPEN

authorHOUSE®

AuthorHouse™
1663 Liberty Drive
Bloomington, IN 47403
www.authorhouse.com
Phone: 1 (800) 839-8640

Published by AuthorHouse 07/16/2018

ISBN: 978-1-5462-5163-7 (sc)
ISBN: 978-1-5462-5162-0 (e)

Library of Congress Control Number: 2018908297

Print information available on the last page.

THANK YOUS &
ACKNOWLEDGMENTS

I'd first like to thank the most high God (Yah-Wei) for allowing me to have the gift of poetry because it indeed is a gift unlike any other, it can influence, lead, support or destroy depending on the person wielding it, because like the good book says "the tongue is like a double edged sword." I'd like to now thank my mother Linda Current, my brother Ronnie Current, my cousin Lansing Lee and my step pops Steven Jackson for introducing me to this thing we call poetry.

Thank YOU THE READER for giving me the opportunity to show you a few Pieces Of Me, it really means a lot. I cant let this book be published without saying thank you to my pops Ronnie Current Sr for his undying support and making sure to question me at every turn so I'd have a level head when I was creating Pieces Of Me. Thank you to my Grandmaw and Grampaw Thaddeus & Billie Sue Snoddy and my Maw Maw & Paw Paw Delbert & Priscila Jackson for their support in everything I have ever wanted to do, so long as I was headed the right way they supported me.

I HAVE TO SHOUT OUT THE MUSKOGEE SOUL SEARCHERS FOR GIVING ME A PLATFORM TO DO WHAT I LOVE!!!

Thank you to a few Marines for their support as well GySgt McCormick, SSgt Talley, Sgt King (RET), MSgt Rogers (RET), 1st Sgt Mitchell, CWO Pierce, MGySGT Castillo (RET) & ALL THE DRILL INSTRUCTORS OF 1st RCT TNG BN/A Co Plt 1002 OO-RAH!!!

LAST BUT CETAINLY NOT LEAST I wanna thank my
wife Katina and our children for putting up with my crazy
open mic schedule and long hours spent on this project,
THANK YOU THANK YOU THANK YOU!!!!!

Special Thank you to STRANGE MUSIC TECH N9NE
& KRIZZ KALIKO. COMMON, BIGGIE SMALLS, AL
GREEN, THE DOORS, AND ANY AND ALL OTHER
MUSICAL ENTITIES FOUND WITHIN THIS BOOK.

You ARE ALL huge inspirations for me.
Sincerely, SOULS INKPEN

MAKE LOVE TO MY MIC

LET'S START THIS OFF RIGHT.
LIGHT FEW CANDLES LET THE AROMA SURROUND I'VE
SEARCHED HIGH AND LOW AND FINALLY YOU I'VE FOUND.
YOU LOOK A LITTLE COLD SO I'LL HOLD
YOU UNTIL YOU'VE BECOME
COMFORTABLE.
I KNOW YOU MAY THINK OF ME AS A KING BUT I'LL BE
A SERVANT TO THE QUEEN AND FOREVER I'LL BE
HUMBLE.
THINK OF ME NOT AS A TEACHER BUT ONLY AS
A POET WHO WRITES YOUR LOVE SONNETS.
SENDS YOU INTO ORGASMIC FRENZIES WITH MY LYRICS
W/MY SLICK TONGUE I'LL MAKE YOUR CUM RUN AND
IT'LL BE ALL FOR YOU MY QUEEN OF HIGH STATURE.
YOUR MERE PRESENCE SENDS ME INTO A RHYTHMIC
TRANCE AND WHEN YOU STARE AT ME THE WAY YOU
DO MAKES ME FEEL LIKE THAT LITTLE BOY AGAIN.
OH REALLY?
YOU LIKE IT WHEN I TALK TO YOU THIS WAY?
WHAT ABOUT WHEN I TOUCH YOU LIKE THIS?
OH YOU LIKE HOW IT FEELS WHEN I CARESS YOUR
HIPS AND KISS YOUR LIPS SENDING YOU SLOWLY
INTO A DOWNWARD SPIRAL OF ECSTASY.
RIDE THESE RHYMES, LET THESE CHORDS
HOLD YOU THROUGH THE NIGHT
ALLOW THESE WAVES OF WORDS TO CURB
WHATEVER IS GIVING YOU ANY KIND OF FRIGHT
AND REMEMBER AL GREEN WHEN HE SAID...
"EVERYTHING IS GONNA BE ALRIGHT"

YOU CAN RELAX KNOWING WHENEVER YOU FEEL LIKE
YOUR IN A DARK TUNNEL, I'LL ALWAYS BE YOUR LIGHT.
OH...MY BAD...
I HONESTLY FORGOT...
YA'LL ALL PROBABLY WONDERING ABOUT
WHICH WOMAN I'M SPEAKING OF TONIGHT.
WELL I WAS SIMPLY EXPLAINING

HOW I MAKE LOVE TO MY MIC.

Adult Aerobics

Have you ever been so in tune with another that as soon
you lock eyes you knew it was meant to be?

This was no ordinary lover
they had a part of your soul & what the love making reminded you of...was

Songs or art or poetry
how the different positions...much like pages...unfold.

I mean, damn this person ain't supposed to be THIS close to me
Kinda makes you wonder what they're made of...love perhaps?

Nah this is pure sorcery.

As you lay next to each other passion arises,
eyes widen and she gives the sign.
"Take me now"
and you grab her up, hold her tightly squeezing life into her body
Y'all roll around the bed making memories
between deep strokes and long heaves
And It feels nothing short of perfect.
allow me to paint a picture...

from the nerd in me
it's that Contra code you entered on NINTENDO,
that warm coat during the winter cold.
that cool pool during the summer heat, that
first time you heard a certain song...
For me it's Commons "the light" or any song I like...its pure hip-hop.

I mean when I gave her head till what seemed like her heart stopped,
her legs jumped, her hands reaching for eternity in sheets
Almost a lovers remake of a painting
You know the one
creating Adam by Michelangelo

Then the heavy sigh of relief cause she's reached her orgasm and her
body drops like the beat...maybe I'm just in too deep...thought that is.

The sound of sopping wet adult aerobics is the same as playing in
puddles in the rain and that back splash completes this text.

Hitting it from the back is reminiscent of thunder and finally the
crescendo of bodily fluids exchanged stretched across galaxies

Etched into infinity and we crumble to the bed like avalanches
enfolding each other in passion {between sheets we made poetry}

We laugh, we try to speak but we know no words can describe
what transpired, THAT coupled with the fact
we're too weak.

So I ask again, only THIS time I'll ask differently...

have you ever been so in tune with someone that
you just KNEW it was meant to be?

©20170618

Brandon J Current
AkA
Souls Inkpen

Be my Instrument

Let me strum your emotions like strings on a violin and make your
heart beat deeply as drums do during the crescendo of a symphony

Please miss lady, be my Instrument.

Let me touch you gracefully as... playfully motioning my fingers up
your vertebrae like Keys on a piano or the notes on a trumpet
I want to make your heart to sink low and your voice to Bellow in
ecstasy baby I want your belly to vibrate as you belt out notes from
baritone through the cuffs keeping you stuck to the brass headboard.

I want you to be my Instrument and oh so much more.
Lets you and I explore sheets and make music,
reading each other like clef notes
You bouncing off of me so much so it reminds the neighbors of Drumline
And together we'll be one band one sound
Under stars we go down
Beneath the moon we create life and the universe will thank
us for creating stars so wonderful they'll ask for an encore so
I'll ask you once more beautiful, sweet, magnificent lady

Could you? Would you be my Instrument...
Just maybe?

SOULS INKPEN

EssEncE Of TiMe

Excuse me miss lady, I was wondering if I could
have a few minutes of your time?

In all honesty it would probably end up being more like days
turned into weeks into months into what seemed like eternity.
So let me start over by asking you for something your
probably gonna scoff at but I'm serious.
See it's a detriment to my being miss lady I need
10

No I do NOT need $10
that would be too small to ask for but what I
need is worth far more than that
I need you to know that so can I have
10?

I see your still lost because I've failed to mention
the reason behind such a question
Beautiful queen of all things poetic and holy

What I've been asking for are the 10 numbers I need to dial so I
can hear your smile over the phone as if I'm hearing stars form.
You've made such an impression I could say I'm second guessing but
we all know from experience we should go with gut instincts so miss
lady, sweet baby, all the titles that could get a man a possible maybe
Could I please get a 10

Sincerely
SOULS INKPEN

FORMS OF LIFE

I wanted to write something new, something for you, something
soulful so I took my pen and allowed my soul to spew
Words like metaphoric streams over falls of limitless
soliloquies flowing freely through these mountains of
hooks and rhymes passing each and every person by.

The father fishes with his son catching the words of the great ones like Poe
The mother helps her daughter pick berries of Harriet Tubman tales in
her hands she is allowed to regale her new-found friends of her tale.
brothers hunt the forests looking for poetic game to gain
so they take well aimed shots of the lost poets getting more
food for thought than the average man can handle.

Some folks just float up the stream of my own dreams, listening to
William Shakespeare they feel freer than the birds in the sky while the
cool waters send forth the voices of def poets like black ice or Gemeneye.

The winds whisper through the soft blades of grass w/the voices of
Marcus Garvey and Malcolm x leaving the trees to wonder what could
possibly be next and the animals of the forest are entranced and intrigued
watching the old folks dance in the spring to the sounds of you and me.

The stage of the world is set as the moon shines its spotlight, everywhere
people pour in from old lows to new heights nothing different all the
same, cause we all came to this spot in this time for this lesson in life.
that poetry is our mother, our father, our husbands and my wife.
Cause to me, poetry is life.

FOOD FOR THOUGHT:

IF I WERE A PIECE OF TOAST
YOU COULD BUTTER ME UP.
IF YOU WERE A STEAK YOU'D ONLY
COME IN ONE FORM...RARE
IF I WERE AN EDIBLE MORSEL TO CHEW I'D
PROBABLY BE A MARSHMALLOW
CAUSE IM SOFT TO THE TOUCH AND GO DOWN EASY.

IF YOU WERE A TOASTER STRUDEL I'D COVER YOU AND
CHERISH EVERY MOMENT AS IF IT WERE MY LAST.
IF I WAS TO DESCRIBE HOW MY LOVE FOR YOU
FLOWS I'D HAVE TO SAY IT REMINDS ME OF TWIX

CAUSE THE CHOCOLATE MELTS EVEN AND THE
CARAMEL STICKS, BUT THE NUGGET BREAKS
DOWN SENDING YOU ON AN OMG KICK
AND IF I HAD TO DESCRIBE YOU IT'D BE THE
FORM OF BANANA PUDDING, CAUSE YOUR
LIGHT, FLUFFY AND PERFECTLY PLACED.
EVENLY BUILT MAKING SURE WHEN I TAKE
BITES (AND OFTEN TIMES I DO)

IM SURE TO GET EVERY OUNCE OF FLAVOR TO TASTE
YOU ARE THE PERFECT BOWL OF CEREAL OVER
A SATURDAY MORNING CARTOON SESSION.
BUT MORE IMPORTANTLY YOUR MY BLESSING.
I COULD KEEP GOING ON BUT I'LL END IT LIKE
THIS, I LIKE YOU TO CYBERTRON AND BACK...BUT
OUR LOVE SPANS BEYOND TIME OR DISTANCE.

Who am I?

I'm just a mind FUCK that took time to look beyond
the books which I was so-called taught from.

The world teaches me to believe none of what I hear and
half of what I see so when I checked into classes I took over
for the professor and not for want of furthering my degrees
but for reasons of not really caring for the lectures.

I get it

You can't stand these gestures, They're uncouth at best.

You want me to sit down at my desk, study the material
handed out and take notes so I can pass or fail the test...

What a jest

I mean you HAVE GOT TO BE KIDDING ME!!!!
wasn't it YOU who said,

"Believe none of what you hear and half of what you see?"

So why is it so bad for me to question the literature
that the teachers try to reach us with?
Oh wait...

I see because so and so said this and that and they have scholarships
to a million schools where they tipped their hats then passed
knowledge they received from a book like this that..

THEY WEREN'T TOLD LIES FROM SOOTH SAYERS???
WELL I CALL BULLSHIT!!!!

I say if you wanna know the Mayans go study the temples for yourself.

If you wanna understand ancient Kemet then travel and see
with your own and don't forget to open your third eye.

Because 9 times out of 9 times these books were written by European
scholars, but I'll call them by the name they should be called

Conquerors.

They take the lands then smudge the truth
They write the books of rewritten history then pass it down to you.
Then they only tell .03% truths and expect everyone to believe it
Well I say if you wanna know the truth then seek it.

How can YOU teach me a history you've been taught by the liars that came
before you then when I question your sources you give ME the boot?
Did I offend you?

I say to know the truth about the trail of tears ask a native.
But know the ones writing history are the ones with the fat paychecks.
We could ruffle feathers and learn and teach the truth
or we could settle for what THEY tell you.

And just in case you're wondering what of this truth I'm really speaking

Just check into why we REALLY celebrate
"THANKSGIVING".

Search for yourself or fall for the lies told to you that keep
us at each others throats and always on the run.

But I'll keep disrupting classes trying to find ways to
educate the masses because if it's pissing off Massa
then I must be headed in the right direction.

And I'm gonna keep pushing.

"TILL ALL ARE ONE"

Inspire

Rely on me.
Get high on me.
What we do is legal so stick by what we do because
we use what people fought & died for

Free speech

And that to me is better than cooked food.

Be live like me
Shoot jive like me
Don't stand on the corner possibly running from to the coroner when
you can be a decent donor of dope lyrics for your neighbors or even
cats from the next state over and even the foreigner.

Be hype like me
Rely on your mind like me
Inspire like we
Because honestly where would you be without poetry?

Letter for the Quitters

Hey you.... sitting there in that chair....YEA YOU!!!

This is dedicated to you

Your stuck between a rock and a hard place

I get it sometimes you feel like you're stuck in gear you can't move
from 2nd to 3rd which means you can't get to 5th clutch grabbing
that split so you can move to 6th and eventually get to 10th

For those of you that don't understand what I
mean that's just the truck driver in me.

This isn't one of those fluff pieces that asks you nicely to
do what you know you need to do because in all honesty
YOUR A GROWN ASS MAN OR WOMAN
And I'm not perfect
hell to be honest I left the house at the age of 23
but that's the whole reason for this piece
I want YOU to be better than me.

And even though I was on stages in foreign lands doing this poetry
It took me until the age of 34 to get serious about doing
a book but I'm here to say HEY LOOK AT ME!!!

I know I know I know sometimes you get caught up and
life holds you back from what you think you want

We all understand what it means to be stuck in the mud but it still
doesn't mean you can't pick up your damn feet and trudge.

Pissing and moaning and blaming someone else for your mistakes
won't get you there so stop it because I'm not listening and no one
else is except for those people that want to see you held back

They talked about Jesus they talked about Martin they talked about you
and they'll continue talking about you until you decide to start walking

And face it you can't take half the people that say they have your back
with you and when it comes down to it half of the half of the half
that I mentioned wouldn't have your back if it came down to it
if you don't believe me leave the house and struggle and it'll prove it.

Ask anyone who's been arrested who was there to put money
on their books and they'll tell you probably no one that they
ran the streets with that helped them to get there
I have a pops that done 21 years so ask me if I care and I'll
simply say no because you decided to put yourself there.

Reality sucks and again this ain't a damn fluff piece
But I'll give you a few words of encouragement to help you get
through it, two quotes from 3 greats in my mind the first one is

"The hardest thing to do is leave everything that you
knew to achieve everything that you want"
~REC & DEC~

AND

"be like water. Now water can flow or it can crash"
~Bruce Lee~

But I urge you to be like the river and be brash
and not be like the lake and sit still
YOU'RE STUCK BETWEEN A ROCK AND A HARD PLACE
BUT THAT DON'T MEAN YOU CAN'T LEAVE AT WILL
Now get on your feet show & the world who's real.

PART I

The Reckoning

It's been over 10 since we met back then and you
have always remained the same to me
Save a few things

The girl I circumstantially met that I couldn't
stop staring at in the visor mirror.
The one I talked to from sundown till the birds chirped in the tree tops.
The one I walked to see in the rain, braving traffic, trespassers and
people that seemed to be losing all sense in the brain
ONLY TO OBTAIN
A kiss.

I knew it then like I know it now that regardless of how irritated
or mad I may get or how much I push at it to go away

THIS THING WE HAVE
Was meant.

with that being said

To Be Continued...

THINGS OF BEAUTY

William Butler Yeats once said
"… all that's beautiful drifts away like the rivers"

I wonder why some women grow old to the fold of
90 and still resemble their beautiful youth.

Maybe it's for them to be blessed with flesh that meshed perfectly
with time because for them it seems to have decided to stop.

Women of melanin descent also natives of this land, not to mention
the Latina at the fruit stand all have one thing in common

They all age gracefully.

Suffice it to be put politely when I say this quote comes from a place of
fallacy cause I swear time has a way of messing with the balance and I
see this in my Mother Linda and Aunt Brenda because they age like fine
wine and CONTINUE to float through time…Much like the river.

My sisters Leila and Canisha and my wife Katina, I can't help but
mention my grandmothers Priscilla and Billie Sue I see it in them too.

These women collectively share a common goal in my
mind's eye, either I'm to be blinded by eternal beauty or
accept the fact that there indeed are real vampires.
I MEAN SERIOUSLY
They never seem to age and as the quote says eventually things of beauty
fade, these women seem to look younger after every single born day.

Maybe it's the Benjamin button effect or maybe it's all
the wine I ingest but I just wanna say to these women I
love you and you all continue to look your best.

Time never seems to cease for the women of beauty in my life, and as
for the quote above...Well it's just that a quote from a man that didn't
have these wonders sitting in front of his eyes when he would write.

Dead Poets Society

ONE DAY I WAS SHOWN THINGS IN PAGES THAT
SCREAMED OUT TO ME IN THE FORM OF DREAMS.

VERBS PLACED ADJACENT TO ADJECTIVES
PLAYING CLOSELY WITH THE NEIGHBOR
KID KNOWN ONLY AS SHORT STORY.

NOT TO BE BORING THEY PLAYED THAT
SICK GAME KIDS PLAY you know the one,

RING AROUND THE ROSIE

AND AS THEY SPUN UNDER THE HARVEST MOON
CARRIED OVER INTO THE SUMMER SUN SOME POOR
SAP WAS LYING COLD WITH A POCKET OF POSIES.

ANYONE THAT KNOWS ME KNOWS ITS NOT LIKELY
TO SIT IDLY BY QUIETLY AND LIE PRETENDING
TO ABIDE AS A TIDE RISES HIGH AND SHAKE
THE LAND OF THE LAKE...but you can call it

POETIC FATE.

SO MANY GREATS HAVE TRAVERSED THESE GREAT
LAKES AND AS I SAT ON THE DOC OF THE BAY I
COULD SEE THEM CAST OUT THEIR LINES REELING
IN CROWDS AT A TIME AND YES IM SPEAKING OF

DEAD POETS

I DECIDED TO REMOVE MY CHOICES FROM VIEW
BECAUSE I COULDN'T BE APART OF SOMETHING
WHEN I DONT SHARE IN ITS BELIEFS.

I CAN'T POSSIBLY FATHOM CLIMBING POETIC FEATS
WITHOUT HAVING HEARD A VERS FROM KEATS.

So I sit...

STARING INTO THE ABYSS PREPARING TO LOSE MY
GRIP BECAUSE A TIDAL WAVE APPROACHES.

I RISE LIKE MAYA, I WAIT LIKE FROST.

I WRITE LIKE POE AS I CLOSE MYSELF OFF
ENSHROUDED IN PRISON BARS.

I PERSUADE MYSELF TO GIVE IN TO DEFEAT, BUT I'LL
DIE ON MY FEET BEFORE I LIVE ON MY KNEES.

SO AS I END THIS PIECE ITS ONLY RIGHT I QUOTE A
GREAT ABOUT WHAT HE ONCE HEARD SOMEONE SAY.

"I once heard an old, old man say, all that's
beautiful drifts away, like the waters."
~William Butler Yeats~
A def DEAD POET.
© 2016

23

LET ME BLESS YOU

LET ME CARESS YOUR HEART THROUGH
SMOOTH INSERTION
LET ME BE WHAT LIES BEHIND THE CURTAIN.

I WANNA SEND POETIC MESSAGES THROUGH INTRAVENOUS
BUT BEFORE YOU SIT DOWN AT MY TABLE I NEED
TO KNOW HOW FAR YOU'VE BEEN BECAUSE
I PLAN ON SENDING YOU TO VENUS.

MISS LADY I'M CERTAIN THIS PROCEDURE OF
PURE AFFECTION CAN CAUSE ELATION IN
PLACES YOU'VE ONLY FELT REJECTION.

LET'S LAY YOU BACK AND BEGIN.

I'M GONNA TAKE AN X-RAY OF YOUR SOUL WITH
MY PEN AND WHEN IT'S ALL SAID AND DONE I'LL
TREAT YOU WITH LOVE BECAUSE I DON'T BELIEVE
A PILL FORM HAS BEEN INVENTED FOR ANGELIC
HEART ACHE SO IF YOUR ABLE TO BE PATIENT
PLEASE WAIT.

I HAVE NO NEED FOR SCRUBS AS I WILL ONLY NEED TO
RUB EVERYTHING NEGATIVE OUT OF YOUR LIFE.

ERASE THE HATE AND ERADICATE THE PAIN
MAKE YOUR HEART MARCH AGAIN TO THE BEAT OF SWEET
CADENCE AND WHEN YOUR TIRED OF DANCING WITH ME
I'LL ASK YOU AGAIN TO...

LET ME BLESS YOU.

I Apologize

I apologize for the rhetoric that the news tends to spew after all
if it weren't for a strong military they'd only be able to say what
the dictator said they could instead of whatever it is they do.

I sincerely apologize for the right to bare arms, that means for
every round I release into whomever crosses my family is ideally
meant to do to them that which they would do to me
cause harm.

I deeply apologize for the emancipation proclamation freeing
my ancestors from enslavement, it meant that the white men of
that day had to get off their asses adjust to a new life, get the job
right in order to make an HONEST dollar instead of beating the
black off of the slaves backs because after all we're all pink in the
middle moreover I apologize if this seems at all like a riddle.

In closing I apologize for apologizing for so much because so little
apology for the nothing you've offered me wouldn't be enough.
You see for me it's not about my sincerity more so about my
sarcasm, so my apologizes are an empty weapon with which I've
handed you and my middle finger is more of a cannon.

Learning to Love

HAPPILY EVER AFTER WRITTEN IN CHAPTERS
OF BOOKS WAS NEVER REALITY.
THE PAGES TURNED READING OF A TITLE EARNED
IS ALL IN THE MIND OF A MAD WRITER
ERGO FALLACY.
THE REAL LOVE COMES WHEN YOU'VE DRAGGED
YOUR KNUCKLES THROUGH MUD AND YOU'VE
COME OUT CLEANER THAN YOU WERE BEFORE.
WHEN YOU CAN STARE INTO YOUR MIRROR AND
SEE THE PICTURE ALTOGETHER CLEARER AND SEE
NOTHING WITH WHICH YOU NEED TO ABHORE.
LOVE DOESN'T COME FROM A PASTOR READING
YOU YOUR VOWS, NOR DOES NOT HEARING
THEM DEEM YOU TO A LIFE ALONE.
IN THE GRAND SCHEME OF THINGS WHETHER
WE'RE SURROUNDED BY PEOPLE WHEN WE CEASE
TO BE ITS NOT WE... BUT ME THATS GOING ON.
BACK TO THE MIRROR MIRROR ON THE WALL
FROM WHICH YOU'LL LOCATE TRUE LOVE.
IT BEGINS WITH ACCEPTING YOUR SELF
BEAUTY, BRAINS, FLAWS AND ALL.
I CAN'T SPEAK FOR THE WORLD ON WHY SOME
LOVE WILL NEVER BE BUT WHAT I WILL SAY
IS PERSONALLY I COULDN'T LOVE ANYONE
ELSE TILL I LEARNED TO LOVE ME.
~SOULS INKPEN~

Candy Lady Of My Dreams

AS I ENTER THE ROOM I SCAN IT WITH MY EYES ALMOST
AS IF I'M SCANNING SHELVES IN A CANDY STORE.

I NOTICE YOU GLOWING THROUGH THE CROWD OF
PEOPLE LIKE YOU WERE A CLERK UNDER THE PERFECT
KIND OF LIGHT. AND AT FIRST SIGHT I WANTED TO GIVE
YOU EVERYTHING I HAD...WHICH CAME TO ABOUT $1.09

I WANTED TO GIVE HER ME, I MEAN SHE COULD
HAVE MY "CHOCOLATE" SWEET GOODNESS
ALONG W/MY "HERSHEY KISSES".

MISSES COULD HAVE ANYTHING I OWNED TO
INCLUDE "RESSES PIECES" OF MY HEART.
AND AS GOOD AS SHE WAS LOOKING, COLORFUL
DRESS TO IMPRESS WITH HIPS THAT COULD SKETCH
A PERMANENT IMPRINT ON THE SOUL HAD MY
MIND STRETCHED LIKE "BIG RED BUBBLE GUM".

MISS LADY LOOKED ABSOLUTELY VICIOUS OR SHOULD
I SAY DELICIOUS, SORTOF LIKE "SKITTLES" AND WELL, I
KNOW I'M SUPPOSED TO BE THE GENTLEMAN BUT I CAN'T
LIE I WAS THINKING IN SIN AND WELL...I MY BRAIN WAS
SAYING "YES, YOU DO WANNA TASTE THE RAINBOW"

NOW THIS COULD HAPPEN "NOW & LATER", HER SILKY
"MILKY WAY" MOVEMENTS MADE ME GO "NUTTY
BAR" OVER HER. NOT TO MENTION HER LAUGH MADE

27

ME LAUGH AS IF IT WERE A SWEET "CARAMELO"
MELODY FROM A "LAFFY TAFFY" DREAM.

YA SEE...

I WANTED TO TOUCH HER "CHERRY FILLED BON BON BODY"
COMING CLOSER TO HER "SWEET TART" HEART AND THIS
FEELING WAS FILLING ME UP LIKE "CREME FILLING" SO
I WENT TO SPEAK TO HER WHEN ALL OF A SUDDEN MY
WORDS GOT MIXED UP AND TWISTED LIKE "TWIZZLERS"
TIED TIGHT IN A TORNADO AROUND MY ASOPHAGUS.

YOU SEE SHE SPARKED INSIDE ME A FEELING THAT HAD
LONG SINCE DIED TILL I SEEN HER STRIDE THROUGH
POETIC EYES AND SHE RE-IGNITED THE FIRE THAT
POPPED LIKE "POP ROCKS" ROCKETING OFF IN MY HEART.

WHEN TO NO AVAIL EMBARASSMENT SET IN, CAUSE
I COULDNT HIDE MY EXCITEMENT. YOU SEE I WASNT
THINKING OF ANYTHING IN PARTICULAR REALLY...
WELL EXCEPT ONE THING AND THAT WAS WELL,
I THOUGHT SHE MIGHT WANT TO GET TO KNOW
"MR. GOODBAR"...BUT LIKE I SAID PREVIOUSLY I'M A
GENTLEMAN AND I'LL KEEP THAT TO MYSELF.

I'D BE LYING THOUGH IF I SAID I WASNT
THINKING OF SNEAKING IN SNEEKERS UP TO
HER LOFT TO WHISPER SWEET NOTHING JUST
TO HEAR HER "SNICKER" AND GIGGLE.

BUT LIKE "M&M" MELTS IN YOUR MOUTH AND
NOT IN YOUR HAND, SHE MELTED INTO THE
CROWD NEVER TO BE SEEN AGAIN.
SO TO THE SWEET SEXY CANDY LADY OF MY
DREAMS, WHEREVER YOU MAY BE...I HAVE ONLY 1.09
TO MY NAME BUT I PROMISE YOU WHAT MORE I HAVE
TO GIVE IS WORTH YOUR TIME, IF YOU'LL LET IT BE.

BEAUTY SLEEP...

TOO MANY TIMES PRINCESSES AND QUEENS
SAY THIS IS SOMETHING THEY NEED.

WHEN IN ALL ACTUALITY SOCIETY SPOUTED
YOU SOME BULLSHIT INDEED...

INTRIGUED BY THE NOTION OF LOOKING BETTER
THAN THE MOST HIGH INTENDED YOU TO BE YOU
DECIDE TO CAKE YOURSELF IN MAKE UP AND SLEEP.

WHICH, IM NOT SURE IF Y'ALL KNOW THIS SO
I'LL SHARE A SECRET IVE KEPT WITH ME...

THAT MAKE UP YOU CAKED UP SMEARS, YOUR EYE
BOOGERS ARE ON FLEEK AND I MEAN THAT IN THE
MOST RUDE MANOR CAUSE FLEEK PER THE DEFINITION
MEANS SHIT, PLUS YOUR BREATH SMELLS OF DEAD
ASS...LITERALLY, SO COULD SOMEONE PLEASE
EXPLAIN TO ME WHERE IN LIES THE BEAUTY?

MY CHILDREN WILL NOT LIVE BY THIS FALSE
PERCEPTION OF REVERENCE BUT WILL LIVE
LIKE PRINCESSES TRAINING TO BE QUEENS.

THEY WILL KNOW THAT THEY'LL NEVER NEED SLEEP
TO REACH THE RANK OF BEAUTY BECAUSE THEY'RE
A PERFECT MIXTURE OF Katina Current AND ME

CAN I BE???

"Say baby, can I be your slave? I've got to admit girl you're
the shit girl and I'm still digging you like a grave…"
These are the words of a poet from the past, please listen attentively,
cause this next few lines will be a living will and testament from me.

You've been the object of my obsession for a few millennia
through distant winds and even when you were held up
by angels and far away from the sins of men.
We were once together in the fields of Mexico, and in the deserts
of Cairo Egypt, I kissed your lips, caressed your hips and
touched you gently with my fingertips ….mmmmmm…

I remember the sweat and the tears you cried when they sold you to
slavery, but I told you we'd meet in this life or the next and I'd get you
back with my bravery, so I say to you these words of a poet from the past

"Say baby, can I be your slave?"

Can I hold onto your being while singing melodies
for our future poetic harmony?
Would you let me be that soliloquy to touch your silky skin, if these
thoughts be a sin, then by all means I'll commit this heinous act
again and again, oh my God please let it be…NO…LET US BE!!!

the beginning of a new family tree and if those evil people
from our past lives try to steal love away again
I'll not do what my ancestors done, instead I'll fight till
the end of the sun and when it is done, we will rest

in each other's arms, your head on my chest, my hand between your breasts our hands intertwined, just let your conscience unwind.

It's almost time, so I ask you again...

"Say baby, Can I be your slave?"

Written by SOULS INKPEN
circa 2007 MCAS FUTENMA

I WANNA

I wanna be able to say I feel what I send out
reciprocate but it feels shallow as of late

I wanna be able to have my better half know that
I gave her my all and know that it's true.

But I'm afraid her "evil twin" won't allow that to come true.

I chose to forgive myself long ago, why can't you forgive you?

I believe in us, more so than you know, I choose to show my
anger, I choose to show I'm secure, I choose to continue to give as
much as I can although I wanna give more, I choose to give long
hugs and touch your skin and kiss your body head to toe.
I choose to say I love you because I want all my feelings to show.

I don't know how to express myself as others do but I continue to try,
even though you'll never see it believe me if this ended inside I'd cry.

You said you wanna tell me mine is the only voice you wanna hear,
the word "wanna" means another is close or is that my inside fear?

I say I love you and your beautiful beyond belief but you can never
accept those words in their true form until your able to forgive me.

Soldiers, Sailors, Airmen and Marines

It's funny how this country loves to use the freedom
of speech but can't stand to hear US speak.

Soldiers, Sailors, Airmen and Marines

It's funny how America can't stand when they see in the media what has
kept this country safe but loves to spout out how they are citizens to the
home of the free and the brave.

Soldier, Sailors, Airmen and Marines

Oh I get it, we're your knights in shining armor when it benefits but when
you see us bitch and complain about how we're treated at the VA all of
a sudden we sound uncouth and the you throw back in our faces that
we signed the contract and knew exactly what that could get us into.
But this Veteran would reply

"You don't know what it's like until you walked 10
miles up the reaper in THIS Marines boots."

I'm not complaining about my service nor whatever Branch others decide
to choose but what I am simply complaining about in this piece is YOU.

YOU WHO HAD THE AUDACITY TO COMPLAIN ABOUT
HOW FREEDOM IS DELIVERED AND YOU WHO WALKED
PAST ME AS IF I'M A PART OF THE PROBLEM OR AT LEAST
THAT'S WHAT YOU FIGURED AND YOU WHO CLAIM
THAT I'M HELLBOUND BECAUSE THE LIFE I CHOOSE TO

LIVE BUT LET ME ASK YOU IF THE COUNTRY CALLED ON YOU WHAT EXACTLY WOULD YOU HAVE TO GIVE. ...EXACTLY...

a silent tongue and not an arm to lift a weapon not a foot to put a boot on so you can begin thirty inch stepping nor do you have the tenacity or the Zeal to deal with what comes throughout a day so when I'm walking down the street all I ask is for the naysayers to stay out of my way.

This is to countrymen and women who refuse to see that because of the

Soldiers, Sailors, Airmen and Marines.

You're able to do the things you do and think the way you think.

So don't thank us because it's really not a need
But if you berate us then it's evil inside you feed.

BLACK PRIDE

I will never wear a dashiki
nah that's just not for me my African pride and Heritage
doesn't lie in the Beautiful different color tapestry

It lies within me and my brown skin and what's left of my
coarse hair and in my high stride and my strong stare

My African heritage lies in Black closed fist raised to the sky being
told "no you can't sit here" and being forced to believe the lies

My African Pride lies in afros and sit-ins and sitting up
front on buses being arrested and being cheated out of
Investments my African pride lies in all the lessons.

I can wait for the revolution because as it's been said it won't be televised
But it'll end up on Snapchat or somewhere else online and the sad
part is all these so-called revolutionaries are becoming sheep

So I keep to myself and wear what I wear and dream
of the dreams of a once living king

But until these sheeple start trying to organize and pull together my
African heritage won't be shown in dashikis signing treaties with feathers

Rather my African heritage will be shown as I am in all black leather.

LOVE IS   POETRY!!

(old writes)
Love is the snake that has bitten me a million times, I've
made girls fall in love with me simply for my rhymes.

This time there is no turning back for I now have what I need
ammo, flack, deuce gear and my pack.

Up Mt Motherfucker I climbed to new heights to be shown the same
level ground that all people walk.... I may as well have let the police
outline my body in chalk, cause I'm truly dead from this love walk.

I mimic the ideas and intelligences from characters in the books
so I have just taken my last brief look and I figure I'd
mimic one so cold he doesn't feel, one who knows pain
and feels it at his heels yet he steps lively still.

Like the vampire Lestat I'll hunt these grounds, why
stop for one when there's plenty to go round
why with just my mere words I could just dine in
every diner and eat at every table for free ... wow it took what
they told me it would to know this is what I must be...
a fucking beast!!!

Why am I lying, why must I be dying, why have I
tried and stood beside myself crying
in the shadows I was as I am in the light.
I understand what it means now to be the
"brother to the night."

Fuck what you've heard I'll relive my dreams over and over again, but
I'll never fight as hard as I have before, I'll never see my heart laying
idle on the floor, I'll never be the last one to walk out the door.

Not the new me!!!

I am and will always be a man … it just took the work of my best friend
to help me shed my skin and like the python I stretch brand new
so I thank you.

I'll Love you, like no other till the light in me ends …. Nevermind…
this is the poem all know far too well, yet it never ends.

So I will say this …. Love is pain and pain is love….

N.D.A.J.

I've never been one to drop a jewel but I'm always the one to
write stars in the skies like Lucy did with diamonds.

I wished I could have half the success that my predecessors had but for
now I'll settle for what I get because even though I'm locally known
I'm globally felt.

Though I've never dropped a jewel I oversaw
the artists that created Orion's belt.

I'm the creature from the black lagoon wearing olive drab starched dickies.

They've tried to destroy and wound and burn and
scorn but after each and every attempt
from poetries womb I'm reborn.

Though I've never dropped a jewel I keep people's minds climbing
Reaching higher and higher for that mine in the sky so after each
and every piece I finish they can feel all the more close to eternity.

Because I never drop a jewel
I harbor as many as I can locate that way when it's time for
me to go and God asks what I've done of late I can say

Father...Father what I've done was kept as
many people enamored as I could.
By presenting them with dreams and goals where only mere trinkets stood.
I've never dropped a jewel rather presented them with gifts of knowledge.
In the end
You never wanna drop anything on the ground for someone else
to pick up rather lead the masses as the son of man did.

PART II

The Quickening

I remember talking about you out loud although we weren't supposed to be

In dreams I screamed about you and to tell you the truth it usually
led to me having to get out of bed to change the sheets

Y'all hold y'alls applause and allow me to be...

Honest.

Hell, we got caught messing around before I left for boot

Lies were told so my life in MY eyes was through.

I took off running but there's a little more of the backstory to our truth,

See I knew then what I still do and its simply this.

Giiiirl I'm gon put a baby in you.

Not like other cats make promises to chicks then slip em the
stick and after the first period is missed off they go into the
wild lost abyss
Naaaaah not this kid.

As y'all well see today, she came to see me leave
and I "came" and ushered life in

And ever since it's been no parting ways like
thunder and lightning or conjoined twins.

When we made love happen it was only then we began to see

Life isn't what we thought it was cracked up
to be until it was about more than

WE

so now we come upon

To Be Concluded...

I m nervous

Feels like my tendons are pulling at my arms and I don't know
what to do with them like Ricky Bobby in Talladega nights.

So I grip my pages, my phone and the mic.

Because if I let go the way my nerves are set up.

I have a run through the door and drop poetry on the floor.

So I try to trap it all inside and keep reading and to
be honest I see my videos and wished I could be like
Lansing Lee and make it all look so easy because
THAT GUY has NO shaky vocals.

NO skipped lines see he tends to stay in "TIIIIME TICK TOCK"
but my nerves are bad and it feels like my breath is choking me up.

So I read all my stuff in one stop because to
breathe would mean to be professional
And that's not me...OR IS IT?

I just wanna read stuff that could potentially top CHARTS make
people's hearts palpate and force the nation's greats to put me on top.
I wanna read professionally in bars, in clubs, on stages & arenas.

Let's be honest the next comet that passes I want the
masses to ignore that bastard and ask questions like

Do you know SOULS INKPEN and have you seen him?

But my nerves hold me back and I keep writing to
stay on track...a few days ago I was blocked but a few
centuries ago had I known how to and got caught.
Massa would've whipped my back.
Would cut off my hands and burned out my eyes
he would even have ripped out my tongue to make me
a lesson to others in what's left of my tribe.

So I have to try to conquer my nerves and be the OVERCOMER,
I have to be the Poetic person I am and be only Invisible to me.

I have to step out of my own shadow and I must move past
this because my nerves are the slave master and I wanna
Give us free.

I have to because I wanna do this Poetry thing professionally.

SOULS INKPEN

Candy Lady Of My Dreams II

Again came a time where I'd met a young lady and I began
bumbling my words mixing verbs with sounds, misspelling
simple things turning similes into smiles all while she was
laughing at me because I began to sound like *NERDS*.

Asking her questions like um...
WHATCHAMACALLIT...
can I have your phone?

Oops I mean your number, like the last four to your
social cause I wanna place mine next to yours after a long
arduous journey where we end up being Mr. & Mrs.

And she just *Snickers*
Her eyes glimmered as she pushed nicely passed
me but I didn't see this as a loss.

I saw it as a second chance at eternity

See I wanted to give her *MOUNDS* of love and happiness

Wanted every morning to start the same with me going insane
because not only do I get to wake up to her *HERSHEY KISSES*
I just woke up heart pounding extremely from dreaming so
deep and all I saw was she meaning it had to be true

This MUST BE LUST ON THE BRAIN...or love

Not trying to confuse you all at all or try to cause conflict but look at
your partner and ask yourself when have you ever felt a love like this?

A love where emotions commit, and heart beats sync thick when
you leave each other for work or bathroom breaks it feels like
your pulling apart from the other half to your *TWIX*?

YOU STAND BY THIS LABEL Y'ALL CREATED THAT THEY...
SHE...AND HE...
IS EVERYTHING YOU NEED
THEY ARE THE REASON YOU WORK SO HARD...
HELL THEY'RE THE REASON YOU EVEN
BREATHE...she's the *ALMOND* to your *JOY* and
he's the *KAT* that completes your *KIT*

That's why you stroll down isles slowly as if to
tell the world this is where it all begins

Because I'm in love with the candy lady of my dreams...

And this is how this piece will end.

SOULS INKPEN

46

Twice Upon a Time

There once was a kid playing in the park after dark
then all of a sudden there was a spark.

New stars born as old ones passed on because at that same time
newborns screamed into this world born either of love or lust.

There once was a boy who played in the park after
dark when all of a sudden there was a spark.

Eyes widened in fear eyes dried from cried out tears,
Staring into distances looking for planets of fantasies
Almost like Cybertron was reachable and the love on Arus
was teachable because he only knew one way to bloom.

A rose from concrete now retreats back into the earth from whence
he came laid down NOT in pain but in laughter because

There once was a boy who played in the park after dark then...

"twice upon a time their was a boy who died and lived
happily ever after but that's another chapter"

The Reason Why

I used to say if I'm not completely happy that I have options.
Drew lines in the sand and I'll be damned if I didn't cross them.

I was so Soaked from the rain in my life and feelings... well I tossed them.
Never thought of the pain that I cause, I wasn't stopping.

Now I'm stuck at a crossroads and tears I caused a few
all my life I wanted love but I went and damaged you.

We were never supposed to battle never supposed to fight.
Our love was supposed to be Sparks like Eternal Fourth
of July Somehow I destroyed everything.

Putting Humpty back together is now my mission I miss the
feeling of romance, miss the smell in the air, Miss the feeling
of accomplishment when I was brushing your hair.
Now it's time to do battle as only a Marine knows how
never give up, never quit
I'll never throw in the towel.
Climb the tower to my Native Queen and slay the dragon at last
Even if it means my death I'm giving all that I have.
It's time to take control of my life time to live like a King It's
time to show my wife the reason we wear these rings.

ZING

Zing that gave rings causing hearts to sing something
like nothing you've ever seen in a movie scene.

Maybe someone you've heard speaking of something quite like this
on the silver screen but like THIS what they have is lacking.

They use words like love as a literal statement, I use the words "more
than life" as a metaphor taking a used to much word and replace it.

Let's face it were altogether strange and not because we listen to
TECH, while others want love like Romeo and Juliet I already have
a love that will make sure I'm guarded...a metaphorical flak vest.
The Morticia to my Gomez splitting Adams creating life.

The magazine to my weapon releasing rounds on hounds
that try to bring strife to our not so perfect life.
A reason to believe this thing can move beyond the ringer, hell
for lack of a better term I believed I found my zing-er

2004 13 August: Im not perfect

It's funny how time goes by, you start to notice the change of the tide.
You want to believe you're the only one but then you find out there's
someone on the side. So, you're faced with two choices fight or flight
and you want to run away but your pride won't allow that to abide.
Yeah, I've had my anger and at times I've cried, but before I
allow you to see that. I commit metaphorical suicide.
But this is not why I've come to this point in life with
these words in text that I choose to write.
I want to start with the date in the headline.
Looking beyond the storm we're in to the sun peeking out
at the skyline I want to go back to a better time.
To when our hearts would start to race as soon as one or the
other would pick up the phone and hear the other say…hi.
I want to look into those same eyes that in my mind (albeit they
were brown) shine brighter than diamonds in the night sky.
Back to when we felt deep down inside something like really
huge butterflies I realize now that I've made you cry one
too many times and for that I eternally apologize.
I still remember chasing after a short Mexican myth, That long hair,
perfect skin, beautiful eyes and not to mention that ass and those thighs.
I refused to allow you to get away because I was
a Lost Boy looking for Tinkers bell.
I didn't care if I had to search every continent on the Earth,
the deepest reaches of space, the hallways of Heavens Courts
or the lowest depths of Hell I wanted you and nothing
short of the commandant was going to stop me.

Then I found out you were Native and you know how to scalp people.
I said all that to say this I later found out how good it was
to be with you and I took it for granted I can't make any
excuses for what I've done only the fact that I was damaged
and somehow I managed to screw up everything perfect.

High Horse

I can't stand people so high on themselves as if they
don't know how to come down to reality
Sweety the way you think coupled with the way you speak
"TO ME"
Is the definition of a grammatical error

To be put bluntly you are completely asinine and not necessarily a necessity
I mean yeah you're cute and you have great sex but you're a want at Best
I should take that word "great" back
No more stimuli no more 4 or 5 or 6x2=12 play

Just a bunch of excuses for why you don't and when we do finally decide to
all you do is Lay

Your ideas of "I'm a bomb ass girlfriend" & "you'll
never find anybody that can do it like this"
sound redundant

Because for me to repeat myself about being unhappy means that
I can find someone that can do it better and be better and think
better and try harder and be smarter so in the words of Ice Cube
"check yourself before you wreck yourself"
But I say check yourself and learn to respect yourself and understand
what you have in front of you because what you don't see others do

Check yourself or be checked yourself because it's not as hard as we
make it seem to have you scanned barcoded and shelved for resale

Now you can keep up with the routine of
"I'm a bad bitch and Nobody Does it Like Me"
Just like I can keep up with the
"Miss Lady I'm just a knight on the chessboard looking for his queen"

In reality you're just withered up and tired still trying to
prove you've got what it takes and I'm just a good man
gone bad trying to learn from his mistakes.

I'll never tell anyone I'm perfect nor will I tell anyone
I'm trying to be because truth be told when a girl with
a big booty and a cute face walk by I look
just like I know a dude with a tight body and
a nice face gets your body shook

I want to tell you that I have faith that we can start over but I don't
so how about we let go of whatever we've done to
each other and go for what we know

Because you are still just as beautiful to me as ever you were before
Somehow we need to get to a place that we understand we mean
more to each other then what we think others do in the streets
because otherwise without that we're doomed to live in the
past and like they say the past has a way of doing a repeat

Basically you need to understand you mean the same to me as poetry.

Love Story

I once met a girl whose name was so hip she had my heart
hopping like Lowriders on a Sunday cruise.

As time began to pass she and I laughed so much we forgot to ask
obvious questions cause no matter what the weather we was

Cool.

She knew I was a Midwest cat but loved the east coast flow
and while she swore allegiance to the west when Twista burst
in the scene she screamed and I sat quietly as if to say...

"Yea, I already know."

Our spirits began to grow.

It seemed as if our time together was coming to a close as I began to
dawn a darkness over myself and it showed in my poor dress code.

No more wrapped rags, only long black trousers, trench coats and
pain.

Ms. Hip called my name but only received my answering machine.

It wasn't until the south bore Scared Faces and Ghetto
Boyz told stories from candle lit rooms

AND

Country boys rocked to my favorite tune of candy painted cars
and hitting switches...A sound so smooth and different

I still kept my distance.

She would call my name from masked numbers known as neo soul and she
knew I was a Prince fan from long before so of course D'Angelo had me
damn near stole, but Musiq Soulchild was what started to drag me home.

All of a sudden I heard a voice too familiar similar
to skittles but different altogether.
His name was spelled out but formed from two letters...
EMINEM.

Some was confused about his candid nature & naming himself
after a candy what type of brother...OH WAIT!!!

WORD?!?!
HE'S WHITE?!?!

YO DOG HE GOT MAD HEAT AND CAN MIC FIGHT!!!

Took me backwards to my Roots, I heard her
voice again and I knew it was true.

she "wasn't worried about where I went or who I saw or what club I
went to with my homies" I wasn't worried cause I knew she had me
and she had me at...
"Ah Yes yes y'all and ya don't stoooop..."

She had me at...
"I grew up a fucking screw up got introduced to the game"

She had me at...
"some of the people appointed to give an opinion never do get it
I want you come on and gobble the jimmy and die...N9NA be

give the remedy and why critics are really the enemy and I can't
stand the way they slam todays gifted effin incredible..."

SHE HAD ME ON THE ROPES FEEDING FRESH BEATS FOR
BREAKFAST AND LUNCH AND WHEN IT WAS TIME FOR
DINNER SHE FED ME THE LEFTOVERS AND CALLED THEM
SAMPLES.

SHE KNEW I NEEDED HER CAUSE WITHOUT HER I
WAS USELESS AND MY LIFE WAS IN SHAMBLES.

She nursed me back to health and I continue roll
with this, My Love, My Boo...My Mistress.

Hip-hop.

©2017-mar-20

~SOULS INKPEN™~

AKA

BRANDON CURRENT

It Was All A Dream

So, I'm sitting in this comfy chair in this ginormous office
sipping Boulevard Bou Lou with Mr. Caribou himself

TECH N9NE

Discussing what I could bring to the table that sets
me apart and so now it's time I start.

Well sir before I begin I'd like to first say thank you for the
artistry you've given because it definitely is different and
got me through lots of the lows that I was living.

Not to mention
I sit in my highs, glass to the sky still rocking to Midwest
Choppers and whatever else comes after on my play list
because regardless of how hip-hop decides to shift

KNOW THIS.

I continue to rep STRANGE MUSIC as you can tell
by looking above the tat on my left wrist,
But that's not what you wanna know is it?
What can I do to make STRANGE MUSIC more appealing?

I know that wasn't the question but I'm just adding
pressure to the rock so when I finish and before you sits
a diamond image I want you to be left knowing

THIS IS IT

What I can bring to the table is myself and my gift which is poetry.

You've been sitting there staring, waiting for me
to reply when all I know to do is write
in rhyme scheme.
I can do what you've asked many others to do in the past and THAT'S
"perform as well as you write."
Read as well as you type.
Look let me stop with all the self-righteous hype,

I've been influenced heavily by this label in my style and the
way I spit Which by the way I NEVER freestyle shit.
EVERYTHING I say is freestyle writ my freestyle script is just that
a free style...shit let me finish by answering the question bluntly,

Krizz said it best when he said

"who am I to you...nobody".

But when its all said and done you will understand why I'm the best.

See Mr. Yates or should I just call you TECH, I'm not gonna
give you a chance to ask too many more questions after
you've asked the most important as the first because THIS is
where I've belonged since I was birthed into this earth.

Some people claim to be STRANGE and some claim to "Have It" but
what I do with a pad, laptop or cell phone and Mic is PURE MAGIC!

I've finished my drink and I have one question for you.

How many more of these do you wanna have
before you say those magical words?
"I wanna work with you."

Yes, this ACTUALLY happened before well at
least inside my mind when I was asleep.

But we're supposed to speak those things that aren't as though they are

And I'm planning on speaking into existence these very things
Because eventually I wanna live life like I do in my
dreams.

LEts TaIk

Yesterday I wrote a piece I couldn't fathom reading in church so how do we as Christians speak in the world not showing them what were worth.

I mean we walk around screaming PRAISE JESUS via Facebook but won't pray for the vagabond on the street…. Trying to get some kush.

And it's funny how I'm saying y'all, but I'm speaking to myself, cause just a few minutes ago I was quoting KRIZZ KALIKO and rapping to Myself.

Then got into my car to hear SHOCK MUSIC.
"How beautiful you are."

I mean it's hard not to
LIKE, COMMENT and SHARE

But I swear theirs a word out there that says, "your burdens I'll bare."

I could be wrong, so please stop me if I am, but before you do
Allow God to minister to my inner sinner man.

No this was NOT how I planned to spend my night
I was on my way to Tulsa to my cousin's album release party.
But hardly, cause this apparently is where I needed to be.

So allow me to address you now as well as the selfish me.

I'm speaking to..

YOU the liar
YOU the judge

YOU the wannabe jury dragging poor souls through the mud.

YOU the dope man, YOU the user, YOU the rider hitting switches,
using riches God gave you not putting it toward your future.

YOU the pastor and YOU the deacon
the ones dressed top to bottom while your flock is
starving like pigeons on empty beaches
YOU.
Yea you, the ones in the front row, let's all take a look at
how we speak, cause if you won't say it in the church what
makes you think you can say it in the streets.

LIVING DREAMS

I remember the night I arrived at MCRD and heard the First Command

"GET OFF MY BUS!!!"

Then all the recruits moved as if we were a zombie hoard but
instead of it being shuffling feet we all exited in a rush.

Stepping onto strange yellow footprints that would change
our lives for the better and amidst all this I somehow kept
wondering how this man in a funny looking cover
Could muster up enough strength to LITERALLY make 1,000's
of grown men scream ultra loud and move extra quick...like this

SNAP

Next came 75-80 days that I don't quite remember.
I mean there's a lot that I do but still one thing that I can't quite figure

During what's known as Black Friday we were dropped to our platoons.
There we met our Drill Instructors and for three months
seem like the holders of our untimely Doom.

We had 5 hats and what that means is 5 men
controlling 87 rambunctious recruits
ranging from the age of 18 and
"you can't tell me shit"
to 28 and
"I've been doing things on my own for a while now
so YOU SIR may kindly go eat a dick".

But again, there's still something I can't really get to stick

I mentioned there were five hats but only four lived with us 24 hours a day.
The senior would visit us at the end of the week
but that's not the reason for this piece.
The one thing that I couldn't then and still can't figure or quite make stick
how those four gentlemen made us all into what we became and
how they made us look at them whenever they screamed
"EYEBALLS!!!"

Because in unison we 87 men screamed
"CLICK!!!"

I remember watching Drumline and hearing the instructor
talk to 'Big Brother Iron Man' and as he scolded him it was
merely meant to remind him of where he'd been.

"How could I motivate a passionate group of my peers?"
Was the question he asked this kid.

I sit back and look at what those Marines, those
motivators, those Drill Instructors did,
And wonder the same thing 'Big Brother Iron Man' did

"How can I motivate a passionate group of my peers?"

And I open my eyes..ook into the crowd and hear the snaps,
claps, and even the shouts and think to myself.

Wow, I just did
I just lived my dream
I guess this is what it must've been like to be one of those
gentleman that made me a United States Marine.

Written by
Brandon Current
AkA
SOULS INKPEN

(A Co. Plt 1002)

(This is one of many ways of saying thanks)

63

Letter to the ones who made me... A Poem.

To the girl who asked for my pencil in 6th grade
KNOWING I WAS USING IT
You knew you could get me to give it which is why
you did it... I needed it for my final grade.

And When I asked you in that little note there was ONLY a YES
OR NO you did NOT HAVE TO LEAVE IT BLANK
Fast forward to what you done in our older days
Needless to say
I hope you catch aids.

To the girls in 7th & 8th grade that made the fat kid
feel he had a chance at love ONLY to say,

"well if you looked like your brothers".

I hope there isn't a tetanus shot created for you
yet and you wither away like old shoes
I would've been good to you.

To the one girl I dated in high school... I want you to live a life
full of everything coming to you for you were a true jewel, A
diamond in the rough, that MORE THAN ENOUGH I just
don't think this world would have been ready for us.

NOW BACK TO THE SLUTS,

To the women I dated after graduation maybe making me fall
for you wasn't in your plans but YOU KNEW THE KIND
OF MIND I HAD AND KNEW EXACTLY WHERE I
WAS HEADED WHEN THINGS WERE SAID!!!

You could've spared me the drama and the I love yous and bomb sex.
We could've been super cool but nooooo you had to bounce
my heart off my head like broke folks do checks.

I hope your feet get blisters like all those ones I
had from every time I ran towards you.
I hope you drown in tears deeper than the Nile river
WAIT
let me paint a clearer picture

.... choke yourself.........

I'm not gonna keep this going too long because I'm
seeing you guys are catching the gist but theirs just some
things I have to say because y'all need to feel this
..............so...............

To the girl that gave me road head while I was wearing my cammies,
had I known you'd given me a VD we never would've gotten married
Oh, and by the way... I HAD JUST COME FROM PT
......Your welcome......
To the men who ended up with any of these wonderful inhumane beings
I hope she shocks you with that powerline of the truth that she done me.
Hope she drops the hammer on your big toe during a deep freeze and
when you're sitting there lonely at night wishing she'd come home
Just know there's plenty like you out there so you're not alone.

P.S. I KID

Momma said

"Momma said there'd be days like this there'd
be days like this my momma said."

But what she failed to mention was what to do when it felt like this
how I needed to go about pulling myself from this rut to get ahead.

Momma also said "Ain't no love in the heart of the city" so I moved out of
town and listened to Bobby B and he made sure to continue the verse she
failed to allow me to see which says "Ain't no love in the heart of town"
so now It seems I'm nowhere bound strapped down to these steady
streams of bullshit all because momma failed to prepare me for this.

Momma…well what can I say
"she taught me everything and everything she
gave to me I always keep it inside…"
but she didn't teach me how to see around my foolish pride so
now I stumble all the time just trying to take it all in stride.

Momma told me when it rains it pours but never mentioned
fake doors and false floors and I'm just "another brick in
the wall" and people you know and love are strange.

NOT those that sit on corner stumps asking for change.

See momma taught me ALOT in those times that she taught me little.

She taught me that every stumble leaves a scar never to be repeated.

Taught me every day like this was to be memorialized

to hold onto it like a eulogy and whenever it feels like it's
happening again you just pull it out and take a read.

Taught me that although there's no love in the heart of the city and
later I found out that theirs none in the heart of town doesn't mean
I can't leave the country...or just love what I have near me
Because HONESTLY what's near me needs more love now than
what they think they'll need later so this creates a seed
where once was a crater.

She taught me windows are like porridge and the doors are made of
soup so whenever I drink from their dirty looks and nasty treatment
it's just a way of making myself better like life's very own Campbell's.

She taught me so much I couldn't stand but to say thank you,
because in the end had you not allow me to learn the hard way
it'd have been all too easy and my life as an adult
ESPECIALLY without you would be left in shambles.

Tired a vent piece

I'm tired of being sick, tired of feeling pain.
I've prayed and been prayed for so much so I feel like God is being strained.

Hooked up to an IV walking to head attached to a machine
makes me wonder if this is the way it ends for me.

Not really, I'm just venting.

I mean I've only been here for 3 days but it freaking sucks
I keep hearing all these honor walks thinking I'm the next to take that bus.

Wife calls me nagging about how hard her life is right now.
And all I can think is if it were you in my position shit wouldn't
be so different because she'd find a way to bitch anyhow.

I can't honor the fallen vets and I keep feeling my numbers
next especially when this pain I feel has carried on 10+
years and the doc says no need for surgery
as of yet.

I wish I could have different words with which to write but I'm
just a stressed and depressed vet but in the end I know
I'll be alright.
Thanks for letting me vent tonight.

Power Of Prayer

This is a piece I'm writing trying not to test your faith
but test your ideas of what's been set in place
so let me set the stage.

The sun sets, and the cracks of the whip cease to exist,
no time for real peace just time to relax a bit.

The master prays: Dear heavenly father please allow
for a fruitful day and my niggers to pick lots.

The enslaved Africans pray: Dear heavenly father, please
free us from bondage or at least make the abuse stop.

The same God hears the two prayers…
or so it's said.

I was always told not to question God and there are things my
mind won't quite understand, so I don't, and I get it.
but what I'll NEVER stop doing is questioning man.

Jesus came to save souls and love us all and we are to
love one another and praise him through it all
lest we fall.

So again I speak of the masters and slave
You beat me into believing in "YOUR GOD" and I have to praise
and pray to him. Well if he loves me like he loves you and we are
all to be as equal why is it then my kinsmen are hung from maples,

streams of blood running down their legs and THIS is the great
staple of the southern hospitality I've been told so much about.

Love one another as god has loved you, love
your enemy as god has loved you

Beat the intransigent slave because they refuse to bare you good fruit.

Isn't this what came from the good book?
Maybe we should take a 2nd, 3rd and 455th look.

I say again this is not written to shake your faith, but merely
have you question man and what's really been set into place.

Nicknames

I've known about a quarter million Miss Ladies and Babies
so much so that jealousy should be the new label because
the way these women act towards each other is shady.

Or Maybe It's because the way my step pops raised me.
He'd see a female and say
"Hey Doll or Hey there Ms. Lady".

I never knew it then, but I'd pick up the swag of the man, myth and
legend that is Steven Jackson but back then he was just my step pops.

I wished I had a watch to rewind time so I could see exactly
when I became this cat that makes women smile the way some
say I do because in all honesty I'm not trying to be...

"Mr. Smooth" or "Mr. let me get to know you"

I'm just trying to do what people seldom do and that's make sure
your day has been made because I understand the bullshit women
go through having seen my own mother go through it x2.

So let's get back to these

Nicknames.

I've already covered Miss Lady and Baby but I've been
remiss to mention one of my all-time favorites and yes it's a
compound noun mixed with painted beauty and sound
so gentlemen say it with me now...

Baby girl.

Conversations would happen, and she'd get to laughing sort of
soft with a deep passion and I'd get to asking questions like,

"What's going on with you Baby Girl?"

And don't let us be in person cause outside you see one
thing but internally I'm eternally nervous.

So I'd flash a smile and bite my bottom lip sort of like I'm
offering you my everything including this poetic gift.

I recall one in particular as I get to the closing of this piece
Sgt Babygirl was one that had me weak.

That title was set aside from the beginning and no one has ever been
referred to by that name since and although I share a similarity to this
chick she was one who gave me reason to have extra deep dark laments.

But this isn't about that now is it…NOOOO it's not
It's merely about a few nicknames.

I was just running over a time lapse in my brain
that made my smile seem vain.

I'm not trying to say I'm a dog by any means, but let's face it I'm a man with
hoe-ish tendencies.

And if you have been addressed by any of the aforementioned names then
Miss Lady I wasn't trying to cause you to feel
any sort of way negatively towards me.

I was merely saying something that would make
your day after ALL it's just a nickname
so baby girl I'll see you around and until next time, stay sweet.

SOULS INKPEN

This woman

I met this woman when she was just 18.
A woman in her mind but a young girl in actions.
Shit
you could tell through her many partnered passions.

She was Melanin mixed with salsa, bachata, liar,
lust, loneliness, English and starvation.

She could craft horror stories out of thin air about how her mother
whom due to legal sanctions shall remain nameless
used to drag her by the hair and BY ODINS BEARD I SWEAR
she could cause you to imagine an infinity where she was
locked away in a tower.

Powerless to stop whatever prison guard is holding her
captive and like audiences watching Schindler's List.

she had me captured.

Raptured away in her abilities to spill words from her soul like

"they're keeping my daughter from me."

And

"Can you believe this nigga kicked me in the
belly?!?! Now whatchu Gon do?"

TO BE HONEST I HADN'T THE SLIGHTEST CLUE!!!

She was fine, and I was just trying to fuck but I failed to mention before
I'd swore I had seen her somewhere Between deep
breaths and the bottom of a glass of wine.

We sojourned to my barracks where as luck would
have it 3 of my best pieces so "ironically" sit.
1)Make Love To My Mic
2) The Perfect Pussy Eater
3) Peter Pans Myth

I went to hygiene and left her to read through, waiting ever so close
to the door just to hear EXACTLY what I knew was coming.

"Giiiirl I wonder if any of this shit is true, he wrote a poem about
eating coochie and I'm trying to see what he gon do to me!!"

I exit the bathroom and allowed the steam to Bellow forth as
if I was Darth Vader coming to destroy the rebels, instead I
showed her my words were worth the read as I began to...
squeeze and pull...kiss and lick god dang this
chick is gonna have me whipped...
she came and asked me to stop and I replied...wait I'm not finished.

Fast forward a few months as she attended EVERY ONE OF
MY EVENTS even though we didn't see eye to eye partly cause
she was shorter than I but still her hard headed ways kept me
awake like words do in my mind when I can't sleep at night.

We would argue then laugh half way through and make up these crazy
weird sounds only we knew... Y'all know the ones I mean, those ones that
"Real couples do?"

We listened to STRANGE MUSIC, watched porn and took
trips all the while she knew I was beguiled by her whiles, hips,
smile, laugh and all that ASS plus all that she'd given me.

And she gave me everything

Well, she gave me everything a man could want or need.
Her heart, her mind, her time, her snap shiiiiit y'all she
loved me so much she even gave me the clap.

She loved me enough to wait till I was asleep to cheat, even waited for
me to leave to sneak, waited for me to take a drink cause she knew I
wouldn't drive if I had then she took the Impala to SD to split sheets with
another nameless figure but for all intents and purposes we'll call him
Capt. Ahab.

She loved me so much she allowed me to believe it was true,
so much so I still believe she did at some point too.

I'm not perfect, not one bit...shit my ol lady I'm married
to now...back then was sending me flick pics

she said
"she can give you what she's giving you but she can't give it you like this."

Ironically after we said the I do's, shit she decided to lay all that
in the grave...but wait, let's get back to the story at hand.

This woman I met in Camp Pendleton was so great she
made sure to wait till the day I flew away to say

"I'm pregnant"

Sent me pics in Kyrgyzstan, had me happy and MOTIVATED
as all hell whilst facing down certain death...let me stop lying,
I was supply so I only faced certain unrest...I digress.

I'm almost done y'all please stay with me on this trip about a woman I
once knew was in love with me as I am in love with this poetry shit.

Let's see time goes by puffing on lies hoping that it gets me high

I was going FUCKING crazy, I mean THIS BITCH WAS
CARRYING MY BABIES AND ALL ON FACEBOOK
WITH ANOTHER MAN ON THE BEACH
WHAT THE FUCK YOU THINK THAT'S DOING TO ME?

HER FRIENDS SHOWED ME THE SHIT, BUT MY LOYALTY
WAS SPLIT SO INSTEAD OF KEEPING IT TO MYSELF
I BEGGED HER TO STOP IF I TOLD HER WHO WAS
GIVING ME ALL THIS INFO FOR MY LAMENTS!!!

She sighed "ok, I SAID OK OK I'LL STOP!"

but little did I know I was going broke all so she could pack up her shit
and leave on a midnight train to Georgia with him...so there I sit.

In Afghanistan tears in one can, pride in the other
begging people for sympathy or empathy either way
I'm just hoping someone would just finish me.

Time goes by STILL puffin on lies hoping that it keeps me high.

Now it's time to fly...

Back to the States I came, seeing families waving to their Marines saying

"Welcome home honey and daddy we missed you, did you miss me?"

And there I was on the parade deck till the hour
struck 23 and along came this...

big pregnant Melanin mixed with salsa, bachata, liar, lust,
loneliness, English and starvation woman...waiting to leave.

days go on and I'm thinking it's we till the day she decided to leave.

But like I said, I believe still to this day that somewhere deep down inside her lies where she found something from which she couldn't hide she actually did love me.

Sincerely
TINMAN
AkA
SOULS INKPEN

Riot Of War

"Some of you know and some of you don't know"

These are words used by dope poet Lansing Lee.

Who knew that these words heard in the 7th
grade would still resonate with me?
See I don't wanna just flood your brain with the who, what, when & where

Rather I wanna lock into memory the dates
worth remembering so you can ponder

WHY? vice WHY NOT!?!?

"They say"
the first bombs ever dropped on American Soil was 9/11.

What about when 1911 weapons we're used to hunt negroes
in 1921 I'm talking bombs dropping to the left and
right while clouds of smoke blotted out the sun.

So when these brave souls prayed to the son they received no
one but a Klansman and a tree from which to be hung,

And that's AFTER the see their aunties and uncles burned
alive while hearing echoes of babies and Grammaws cries.

How black hands rose tired and hot, while white hands
reached down NOT to help but to continue the plot.

Please don't Ssshhhhhhh me or try to shut me down.

I'm merely breaking down the bullshit you've been told vice
the truth that's LITERALLY LAYING AROUND.

The American military used planes from WWI and
dropped bombs on Tulsa smoke blotting out the sun
While troops carried out orders.
In the end the Brady theater stood tall where once
Banks, grocery and shoe shops were.

But don't believe me, do your own research for once.

Fast forward to 1923 just TWO YEARS AFTER THEY
ATTACKED one of Oklahoma's greatest cities.

Rosewood was the name of a small town in the middle of Florida.
A white woman beat up by her extramarital boy toy made
it seem as if a negro raped and stomped on her.
The white populace located, closed with and LYNCHED
ENTIRE FAMILIES all the way down to babies
barely able to reach the top of the crib
SO
Long before pearl harbor, long before we stormed the beach,
long before McVeigh blew up a building in OKC.
These domestic terrorists were hunting people
that looked like YOU and me.
So the next time "they" wanna tell you about the first bombs
dropped at our boots, look them in the eyes and say,
I know the truth, do you???
SAME SAME BUT DIFFERENT

We're all cut from different cloths and all told different stories of
"who we are and where we should be"
When in fact we carve our own paths to which we discover our own dreams.

Her mother wants her to go to prep school and be competitive in cheer
While she just wants to do ballet and skate board and
be comfortable around her collective peers

because for HER there is life here

His father wants him to go off to college and be the next Thurgood Marshal
All he wants is to join the Marines do his time
in the fleet and he keeps screaming

POPS I DONT WANT YOU TO SEE THE NEXT ANYONE
ELSE, I JUST WANT YOU TO SEE THE NEXT STAGE
OF MY LIFE AND SEE AN EVEN GREATER ME!!!

See we're all cut from different cloths, she grew up on the
good side of the street while he grew up in the slums.

She only has to worry about the problems of class.
While he has to worry about making it home
without staring down the barrel of a gun.

But although we're cut from different cloths
we're all a part of the same fabric.

Made to praise the King and let the rest of the world have it

Do magic with our words and show those who are lost
The way

We each have a destiny to fulfill, it's just taking the
journey that puts those opportunities in your way.

You can be great at cheer and do wonders in the Marines but if God
isn't a part of your life then your destiny will be just that...
a short lived dream

I say this in closing as I hope my point was made
When we die we have 3 important things on our stone to be remembered...

1) The day you were born
2) The day you were taken

3) A dash in the middle

You could Embrace your destiny and help others to see their potential, or you can live hindsight 20/20 and watch the rest of the world around you.

We're all cut from a different cloths but made from the same fabric let the creator be your guide and watch him work his magic.

MY BROTHERS

My brothers all told me to be careful...I listened with a
spiteful ear and a smiteful smile a cross my face.
Had I known the truth behind the lie would be the way I was
supposed to be or play the game how I was played...
would I have ended up this way?

My brothers told me to be careful who I let have my heart, well I
listened intently with a permanent stain from the start, should I have
resparked the light inside my life when I was given the final order
after three months of torture, should I have reacted so seriously?

I sit back and notice these things my brothers told me
unfolding before me and all I can do is sit and say....
Damn.... My 1,000,000,000 brother were right.

They all asked me was it worth the fight, I said yes in reply.
I would have it no matter the hardship, no matter the struggle,
no matter the pain, and I'd be the one to suffer in the rain, feel
the winds of the tornado, feel the floods of the rivers, while I'm
lost in the tranquility of my tears I fear that substance
Is but a refilling of my souls ink pen
it will strengthen me to a point where I can't feel, and
never again will I say what I said, never again, will my
heart be misled...cause my motivation is dead.

I can fly on golden wings and feel a high from the earthly things
that sing to me their worries, yet if my vision is blurry and the

bird has a blinded eye... we may have to settle for the ground as
oppose to the sky and walk through this terrain and feel all the
mortal pain, knowing what I know now, I wish nothing back,
nothing changed, nothing.... Everything stayed the same.

It was worth the fight, worth the pain
it was worth every struggle that made me go
insane, it was worth the end results
it was worth the truth.... Cause for almost a
year...I found what I needed in you.

I found I could live in the light, I could have what I wanted and more....
So to my brothers, I'm done fighting in this war, I'm done going street to
street, house to house, but yes this was worth it ... now my pen is dried out.

So to my brothers I ask you this ... can you go as far as I can and still exist?

Refill my ink, because I refuse to let my poetry exist.

I'm done with this.

$U pO +

This is a piece dedicated to those that say action
words yet their words don't reflect action.

It's one thing to say I am sick but I like your shit and
another to say I'll show up then when time comes.

"Aaaaaah man see what had happened?"

I'd rather you do what I did
JUST SAY YOU CAN'T MAKE IT.

But see I get it, we're supposed to be defeated when in all
actuality it's you who miss out on the gems and stems that
grow flowers but it's all good because we'll feed...THEM.

The ones who show and the ones who show with them.

See they are our audience not those like you and for
conversation sake we'll call those folks
nem.

I suppose I could relate to those that say they're gonna do one
thing then decide to do something different, because I've said
I was gonna lose weight for what seems like a century.

So it's all good y'all stay over there and we'll stay over here

And to paraphrase one of my favorite rappers what that
describes what I'm talking about short and sweet.

When this book blows up and these shows close up

or

"when we come back for holidays and cruise the streets just tell your ugly ass kids you went to school with me".

This is the story I wish to share...
Here goes a tale of two thieves
From two different seams and two very different places
of being yet brought together through ROTC and a child
who would grow to be the epitome of Poetry.
This is the story of the times of parties and mancala, when
being a shot caller was the ultimate slang and we would
bang on a boy who wanted to throw them thangs...
We were one in the same.
This is the story about how this entity came back from the dark, who
sat out in my parking lot and stayed with me till the sun was brought...
who worked at Taco Bell from start of the clock till it stopped.
This is the story of two very same people who barbequed at the lake,
swore to each other to never be fake and who ate off the same plate, whose
throw up I scraped with the shirt off my back, who I told was kin from
another skin... Man if this isn't something special I dunno what is.
This is the story of how we fought, she bitched, I complained yet
The Wiz
wouldn't be the same without this person.
If you know a person like this cherish what you get cause I swear when
shit hits the fan she's your towel, when your sweat hits your face, she's the
hand to wipe it, when the blood runs from my nose she's my napkin...
and when things are going bad... no matter what direction it's in...
She's my Best Friend

The Con-versation

.................thug to veteran.................
See, I'm a Kombat Vet too
This concrete jungle is where I do all my battles.
You can see all the things I've been through from
the flag on my head to my red laced shoes.
See I'm a Kombat vet too.

All these people
I SAID ALL THESE PEOPLE!!!
Fight for the same thing
I mean basically we're like a militia, a small army
nah nah fuck that we're some straight up
Street Marines.

You move to our Hood and you gotta pay dues, we protect
you from the enemy on the next block over

And if you refuse well we're the enemy right next to you.
See I'm a Kombat vet too.

I still remember them niggas had came around the corner
spraying and killed that baby and the homie "lil blood game" but
it's all good cause we took the war BACK TO EM Y'ALL.

SEE WE SPRAYED AK, 9MIL, SHOTTY, AND
TECH NINE BULLETS when we drove by.

Shit, they didn't care about none of ours so who
gives a damn about any of them?

See I'm a Kombat vet too.

You went to Afghanistan, Didn't you?
These streets are ALOT like that but different and
I'm just trying to do my part...like you.

........................MARINES REPLY........................

Yea, I'm a combat vet, I've been to a war zone.

Never thought that war would follow me home...
well except in my dreams and old bones.

I moved to this neighborhood because I wanted something different, not
because I wanted my heart rate up because I'm back in the same conditions.
You offer a protection but keep the people around you living in a prison.

Some of them want out but you put your foot down saying ain't nothing
changing while being the same poison you saying your fixing.

What exactly does it matter, I can't see the latter because all you're
doing is giving the hood to the devil on a silver fucking platter.

You say "lil blood game" was murdered so you done a drive
by with lots of rounds...well one of those came right past my
head and hit my uncle in the next room now he's dead.

Another stray flew past my house, struck and killed the old man while
he was sitting on his couch...same one you talked to yesterday

3, 4, 5 more whizzed past hitting cans and stands light
poles and T.V.s while these kids see this and realize it's
not on a 60" flat screen this is a horrid reality.

You make accusations about someone and 3 people get shot, we had intel
that bad men were in an area and we went to work and yea targets got
popped, but we made sure to do our best to keep the innocents alive.

While you just pray and spray not realizing your killing those you
swore to protect physically and if not...they're still dying inside.

And while I'm at it, you're doing things you KNOW are illegal
And when the boys in blue come you make the "so-
called villagers" speak up for you.

Well that's not me, so I'm saying this to you.
Get off my porch and get off my lawn cause this
combat vet won't run from or protect you
but I will shoot.

See theirs lots of ways this conversation could play out,
But it's up to you so called gangstas to decide to speak out.

You say this is your hood and you say you own the block,
yet you live in your mom's house still waiting on her
money to buy you some new drawers and socks.
Educate yourselves and be better than the generation before
because the road to hell is paved with good intentions.

And it doesn't have a revolving door.

SOULS INKPEN

PART III

The Happening

Two dates happened that made me happier than
a fat kid in a cheesecake factory

And those fell in 2013 & 2015

Two beauties graced the earth brought to you by their momma and me,

One born 1 July (54) and the other born 8 June (11)

Both have my big ears and my smooth swoon, but they also have their
beautiful mothers face so it's no mistake they completely take over a room.

I'm talking about my baby girls Josilynne and Letti.

They can smile and laugh and cause all sorts of havoc and the world...

Well they'll just let them have at it,

I'm not so easy at letting them get away with it.

I believe in a certain sense of order and while they DO HAVE
ME WRAPPED AROUND THEIR HEARTS.

I make sure they know there's a line and they should
be careful not to cross that border.

I'm not afraid of whooping and rearing them in the direction of success

For I know if I don't then someone else will take them away and
I'd give everything I had to make sure that doesn't happen.

Even give up the last beat in my chest.

I wished words flowed different, so I could better explain my mind state

But I'm excited for what's to come and honestly, I can't freaking wait...

Well today's the day.

The Reasoning

I remember being angry saying how I'd never have another baby

My wife drove me 90% crazy and she kept pushing
and pulling my brain in different directions,

But through it all was a lesson.

It had to be her, couldn't be anyone else
I couldn't bare seeing my kids living with someone else

Couldn't have two baby mothers separate homes for my little bits
So, when times got rough I chose to find a way to make it stick.

Now two kids later, couple of cats and pit bulls we've
stumbled upon the next entry in this adventure

And its name is YOU

Thaddeus Lloyd Current (49).

The Heir, the one to carry on the name
All our children are the reasoning behind the love and the pain.

For you we've pushed through and for you we'll continue to fight.

Our family is complete now and for you all I'll try
harder to live more healthy in my life.

The numbers you've read are more than mere numbers to me
See these numbers are the very minutes all our
children came out and began to breathe.

How I ll Hurt You

Good evening miss lady, I saw you from across the
room and I wanted to introduce you to
Every man you'll ever know as well as those you already do.
BAR KEEP!!!
She'll have whatever you've been giving her mixed with my
charm for her elixir and just before it hits her we'll be laid
up on some distant peninsula known as her emotions.
Can you see the picture…No?
I'll just keep painting pictures of figures YOU and I dancing in
meadows of beautiful flowers and travelling across distant oceans.
Let me stroke your ego by saying how absolutely beautiful you are and
there isn't a person on the planet that rates to be in your space because
How high you set the bar
Anyone else trying to reach it is merely subpar but I
wanna take it slow so let me not get ahead too far
I'll stroke your wrist calling out your favorite perfume mists while caressing
your hips slightly cause I want you to watch me watch you as we speak
Take notice to my eyes watching your full voluptuous lips
I can remember every word you're saying from the way you pitch your
words to the very way you annunciate and place every syllable
Miss lady I want you to know I am here with you.
We stand up, hands intertwined my eyes meet yours
at the very second yours meets mine
Almost as if we're of a like mind.
Alas, I've left one piece of the puzzle out which I plan to
collect in a bit, but let me be generous and leave a tip.

Now YOU I mean SHE and HER and THEY and WE can
step lively across the vast countryside of our minds eye where
all is permissible and all is kept between WE and I.
YES...WE AND I
I, much like any lion chooses to be part of a pride and this
heart throb of a ride takes no tokens for which to play.
Remember when I said I had to leave a tip? Well now it's time YOU...
oops I mean SHE and HER and THEY and WE...to pay
What's that you say? You have no currency for which you can pay this due?
It's all good miss ladies, I'll take your emotions as collateral
and leave you wandering in shambles disappearing
into the abyss as night has come to it's end
You realize well after you've given your all and
you feel is the regret of being used
Don't be mad at me ladies for I'm just being a
king and this is merely a script of
How I'll hurt you.

Memories

My memories are filled with cherry tobacco out of a pipe and old whiskey dances from a cool old man that meant the world to me.

He would get tipsy and pass out money but DON'T GET IT FUNNY cause when he sobered up he called the house and said bring it back.

I remember tube TV and sitting...head cocked...hands in lap as we stared through the Gunsmoke deep into the eyes of the one Miss Kitty Russell

Always had that calendar on the wall we boys would try to peak through and stories of the old days but I couldn't listen because I was so captivated by his voice

He was a strong dude worked on his own vehicles, worked on his own house, knew what to do when things started to go south at least this is the man from my account.

Car rides were always cool cause we either rode in silence or listened to the blues hell that's partially how I became so DAMN smooth.

And I can see too, how women would fall for the gray eyed wonder, voice was like wind and rolling thunder, yet he kept to himself and done the work no one else would wanna.

Every student knew that janitor Thaddeus had your back but don't get to actin a act cause he could also snap.

I have so many missed memories of how he tried to teach me, but my LEO pride and teenage knowledge basically said

"Maaaaan miss me with the rhetoric".

But at every turn I had to admit it Grampaw you
were right, and I thank you for the lessons

Most of all I thank you for letting me ask endless questions, I
thank you for showing me through the mistakes you made that
the road could be rough but it depends on the way you pave

I thank you and remember you for all the things you done to teach us

But what I remember most is the western, always the westerns
Between us

❧

I remember westerns always with the westerns.

Bonanza, western books on the night stand, cowboy hats, the click
of boots walking on the floor If only I could hear it once more.

It's been 26 years and it seems like just yesterday I was sitting on your lap
listening to you talk and make promises that weren't for you to keep.

I remember running, laughing hoping you would catch
me when I tripped, and you always seemed to.

I remember your laugh it will hopefully be something that
will never pass and I remember watching all the shows
from Buffy the Vampire Slayer to Highlander and Stargate
SG-1 and let's not forget all the Sylvester Stallone.

I remember hearing the golden oldies and singing along on
the way to Grandma and Grandpa Durham's house.

I remember games we played like hawk and kings on the corner,
which was always hard for me to lose But I usually did

but all these are memories of a small child and teen.

As an Adult it's a lot harder for me to say because I can't see your
face, hear your voice or get the hug I so desperately need.
it's now been 11 years and my heart will never be full again.

I will Love you for an eternity and a day, but you will forever
fill my mind with everything I did and didn't get to say.

~SOULS INKPEN~
Ft. K Current

Printed in the United States
By Bookmasters